THE BOOK OF \
AND POR⌐

by John Kemp
drawings by McLean

Nigel J. Clarke Publications
Unit 2, Russell House,
Lym Close, Lyme Regis,
Dorset. DT7 3DE
Tel: 01297 442513
Fax: 01297 442513

Web site www.njcpublications.demon.co.uk
e-mail mail@njcpublications.demon.co.uk

ISBN 0 907683 32 0

Contents

PART I

WEYMOUTH

THE EARLY YEARS

A canon ball lodged high in a wall in Maiden Street close to the harbour indicates very clearly that what is now called Weymouth was once two towns; Weymouth on the south of the harbour, and River Wey and Melcombe Regis on the North side.

Pre-historic man settled here and prospered, since the ecology of the area · a small, 3 mile long stretch of river, shallows, marshes and cultivable downland · suited him well.

The river and its haven, sheltered from the prevailing SW airstream by the huge bulk of Portland and the Chesil Beach was certainly used by Bronze and Iron Age people, and long before the Romans invaded Wessex in AD 43 they and others had made use of its favourable position for trade with Europe and the Mediterranean.

During the Neolithic age the inhabitants had built long barrows on the surrounding hills, Bronze Age folk constructed round barrows, and from 600 BC the developing culture of the Iron Age built the hill forts at Maiden Castle, Abbotsbury, Charlbury and the Verne on Portland. In the years following the Roman invasion the victors and Romanised Celts populated Weymouth and the surrounding area. The haven of Weymouth and other landing sites along the River Wey at Radipole were served by a Roman road leading to Portland from the important town of Dorchester.

The shape of Weymouth and Melcombe Regis has been changed enormously over the years; in Roman times Melcombe Regis was little more than a sandy spit of land. But Weymouth, which has yielded evidence of Roman occupation, was probably served by a road running from Broadwey and Radipole, west of the lake, which probably continued on to Wyke Regis and thence to Portland. The Romans made much use of Portland stone and the Isle was quite strongly settled by them.

1000 TO 1348 - WOOL AND TRADE

During the decline of the Roman civilisation and the emergence of the Saxons over the next 1000 years both towns continued to grow, retaining separate identities. In 1024, Edward the Confessor gave the manor of Weymouth to Winchester, then the capital of Wessex, and in 1110 both Weymouth and Melcombe Regis were referred to as ports. By 1280 Melcombe Regis was incorporated as a borough, and it was at about this time that disputes over the use of the harbour began, each place claiming infringement of rights by the other.

Weymouth's charter as a borough was not granted until 1318, but by 1319 Weymouth and Melcombe Regis were granted the right to have two representatives each in Parliament. For towns so small even to have one parliamentary representative was remarkable, let alone two each. This was still a remarkable anomaly even in the 18th century.

The Town Hall of Weymouth 1825

The importance of these two ports is reflected in their being able jointly to send 20 ships to Edward III's siege of Calais, which compares favourably with Bristol's contribution. The trades which had so stimulated the growth of the ports were in wool exports and wine imports by Melcombe Regis and Weymouth respectively. It is interesting to note that Weymouth's earliest record of trade was in wool, but the handling of this commodity, a staple was later taken over by Melcombe Regis by the granting of a Royal Licence. Wool, incidentally, was more than a staple export or a staple commodity; for centuries it had been, and for centuries it would be, a cornerstone of existence. In every hovel or home it was spun and woven, and what was not worn was sold. It was, next to food and shelter, the most important and time consuming aspect of everyday life, and was worn in some form or another, by all parts of society.

A few observations on other aspects of life are not inappropriate. Housing, for the majority, was often wood and thatch or mud, straw and thatch, and only occasionally of stone; floors were of beaten earth. Several generations would share accommodation and share work also. From the age of 4 or 5 years onward children would be workers, gleaning wool, or berries and fruit, firewood, and would be trapping birds in stone traps. Wheatears (known locally as 'snorters') were much valued, but any animal was fair game. Infant mortality was horribly high, illness and disease were rife, and work was dawn to dark. Fish was a major part of the diet, and a summer surplus would be salted for the winter. Cooking was done in pots over open fires, vegetables few, herbs and hedgerow plants much in use. Scurvy and malnutrition were common winter ills. But holy days were not infrequent and Sundays were relatively happy days as it was not until the times of the Puritans that Sunday merriment was banned. But there was no lack of real piety. In the lowest classes people had few rights, and women had no rights at all. Her husband was chosen for her and she merely a bearer of children and a workhorse, while her peasant husband was, in the worst cases, the property of the manor.

4

1384 - BLACK DEATH

The Black Death arrived in England via Weymouth in 1348; this plague, spread by the rat flea, was cataclysmic, with as much as a half of the kingdom's population dying in two years; but it did have the beneficial effect of giving rise to a cash economy, whereby the serf became a wage earner. Labour at last was valuable.

Life in these two towns was fraught with dangers other than the plague. Raids by the French and others were not infrequent, so in 1377, when Charles V of France had sacked and burned Weymouth down a chapel was built on the high ground overlooking Weymouth on what is known as Chapelhay. Until that date worship had taken place at Wyke Regis Church, a practice which left Wey-

The Harbour from Nothe Esplanade

mouth unprotected at those times. The present Wyke Regis Church dates from 1455 although the list of incumbents goes back to the early 13th century. The mother church of Melcombe Regis was at Radipole, until 1606 when St. Mary's Church was first built.

By the 16th century the essential elements of both towns were established. A great deal of land had been reclaimed from what is now called Backwater and Radipole Lake and the basic street plan of Melcombe Regis was in existence. Melcombe Regis offered far more scope for land reclamation than Weymouth and its very flatness destined it for its role as the future town centre.

Trade at this period was not at its most brisk, but trade links went further afield and many men of humble origin took advantage of this and became, on occasion, wealthy merchants. This gradual increase in wealth gave rise to more substantial buildings, such as Weymouth Town Hall below Chapelhay, which survives, albeit much modified, today, as does the Tudor house in Trinity Street. Accompanying this increase in wealth and to guard Portland Road with its ships and valuable cargoes, Henry VIII caused Sandsfoot Castle (1539) to be built, with a counterpart on Portland, while the Nothe (corruption of nose) continued to be provided with guns and a look-out.

THE ARMADA

In 1588 the Spanish Armada made its doomed assault and several Weymouth ships were involved in the confrontation; a squadron flagship, the San Salvador, was brought into Weymouth Bay and was looted, with only an iron bound treasure chest surviving to end up in Weymouth Museum. Several Weymouth ships of over 100 tons were involved in a major battle off Portland, which gives some idea of Weymouth's growing importance. At the time, nearly 100 fishing boats also based here.

1606 THE TRADE IN EMIGRANTS

By 1606, when James I granted a new charter incorporating both towns a bridge had been in existence between the two towns for some time, replacing the original ferry.

Trade was now becoming even more far flung and Weymouth enjoyed not only trade links with the American and West Indian colonies but also played an important part in conveying emigrants to these new lands. A voyage to Barbados, for example, was recorded taking just six weeks from Weymouth, but such fast and uneventful trips as this were regarded as miraculous. More frequently these journeys consisted of vile discomfort, rife disease and foul food and drink. A rector of St. Peter's, Dorchester was one who went and helped to found Massachusetts as did John Endicott in 1628, who became its first governor.

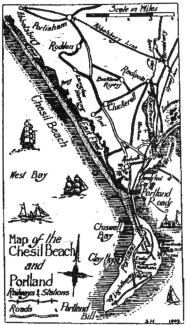

Map of the Chesil Beach and Portland
Railways & Stations
Roads

Reasons for the increasing numbers of emigrants were many; religious persecution was one reason, but population pressure was another. The population of England around 1620 was approximately 5 million, and famine and pestilence had accompanied this recent population explosion. Land hunger was yet another, and, incredible as it may seem, a further incentive to settle in New England, say, was the scarcity of domestic firewood and fuel in England. Several severe winters had also caused havoc.

As well as 'exporting' people, Weymouth and Melcombe ships were involved in importing immigrants from the continent where persecution and living conditions were even worse than here.

6

In the early years of the 17th century smallpox, plague and famine were once again having the effect once again of slowing the previous population increase. The average life span was 40 years or less, and infant mortality remained high, as did death in childbirth. Living conditions in small towns like Weymouth (this name from now on incorporates both Melcombe Regis and Weymouth) were very unhealthy. Sanitation was non-existent and depended on rain to sweep all imaginable types or refuse into the town ditch, streams or sea. Drinking water was obtained from wells, particularly on the Melcombe Regis side, and springs on the Weymouth side.

THE LAYOUT OF THE TOWN

One of the problems an estuary town like Weymouth had to face - and it is the same today - was silting up, and mention was frequently made to dredging operations. But dredging had a beneficial effect in addition to keeping the harbour navigable; dredged material was used to reclaim land from the Melcombe Regis side of the Backwater, and it was the direct result or reclamation that Weymouth grew to become what it is today. From just beyond where the King's Statue is today, along the present Esplanade was a strip of land called the Narrows, bounded on one side by the Backwater (Radipole Lake) and the sea shore on the other side.

Measures were being taken at this time to prevent Weymouth from becoming a squalid shanty town; only freemen were allowed to trade in the town thus ensuring that as far as possible they were not undercapitalised. Other people were allowed to trade by a specially purchased licence. Products from outside the town could only be sold in the market in St. Edmund Street. The harbour with its piers and wharves was being properly serviced, and some money - but never enough - was being spent on the town drawbridge. Vantage points and gun emplacements were also being maintained. Close to what is now Hope Square on the Weymouth side was at that time Ope Cove, where ships requiring ballast could be served. The Old Rooms, its building still in existence backed onto the harbour at this point. Because of its hilly terrain Weymouth was already less developed than Melcombe Regis. Its most bustling street was High Street, long gone, but it's course was along North Quay, ending near the Town Hall previously mentioned; its Harbour Master's house was where the Municipal Offices now stand.

Weymouth Harbour 1825

THE ENDING OF PROSPERITY

1645 was the year the cannon ball lodged in the house wall in Maiden Street, and the Civil War had been in progress for three years. The ball was probably fired from the fortification on the Nothe (called Nothe Fort) as a result of the short lived Royalist occupation of the Nothe in an attack on the Parliamentarian held Melcombe Regis. That siege lasted for three weeks, and brought to an end the power of Royalists.

From this point on Weymouth's fortunes were on the decline; ships were larger and sought larger ports, and the damage caused by the Civil War, and general neglect, put a great strain on the town's resources. Entreaties to Parliament produced only meagre relief. Exports of wool were on the decline too, as finished cloth took over from ports closer to the areas where weaving was carried out on a larger and more profitable scale.

One of the most horrible incidents of the late 17th century was the outcome of Judge Jeffrey's trials of those who had been involved in the Monmouth Rebellion. The severed limbs and heads of those victims were paraded from end to end of Weymouth and were hung at designated places.

The carrying of convicts and coal was now keeping Weymouth at least in business, which was further helped by re-supplying North American colonies, all of which necessitated the building of warehouses on the Melcombe Regis side of the harbour.

Another increase in 'business' which much employed local boats was smuggling, with Lodmoor, North of the town, being a favourite landing place, while Preston and Radipole had the reputation of being places where contraband was stored prior to selling; Fleet Church has a similar reputation. Down the face of White Nothe (a prominent white cliff north of the town) was the precipitous track mentioned in Meade Faulkners's book 'Moonfleet'. Speed was essencial in moving smuggled goods from the beach to 'safe' storage places. Kegs were strapped todether and slung over the shoulders of porters who were known in the trade as 'flaskers'.

In 1713, coinciding with the end of war with France, a new bridge was built, again with a drawbridge; and Wyke Regis, to celebrate the end of that war spent just over El for a bonfire and beer. Fortunes were perhaps looking up again, for early in the century that tireless traveller and writer Daniel Defoe wrote of Weymouth as being a sweet, clean, agreeable town!'

8

The Harbour, looking seawards. c. 1890

1700 WEYMOUTH AS A RESORT

By the mid 1700s Weymouth was becoming a resort, following the example set by Ralph Allen, a wealthy Cornishman, who adopted Weymouth as a place of recreation. He was a very influential man and with his many friends was instrumental in making Weymouth a socially desirable resort. His friendship with the future George III's brother, the Duke of York, reinforced Weymouth's social importance.

A map of 1774 shows Melcombe Regis well developed, but with very little building along the present Esplanade. It also shows the very pretty St. Alban Street was then called Petticoat Lane. Land was fetching high prices and reclamation from Radipole was going on apace. In 1780 George III's younger brother commissioned for himself the building of Gloucester Lodge to stand in its own ground it would have had · and still has · a fine view along the sands, dotted at that time with many bathing machines. It should be observed that the fad of sea bathing was not confined to bathing in it; it was recommended that it should be drunk as well!

It was in 1789 that the visit occurred that was to confirm Weymouth's place as a fine resort. George III, recovering from a bout of illness, made his first visit here, staving at Gloucester Lodge for 10 weeks. So frequent were his visits thereafter, and so popular did Weymouth become, that by 1800 buildings were beginning to stretch along the Esplanade, and sea defences were being built to protect it. Until that time much of the sea front was used as a rubbish dump, but then this practice ceased, and by 1812 most of the Esplanade was in existence.

9

Statue of George III unveiled 25th Oct. 1810
'Painted in present colours 1949'

1805 saw the last visit of the king, and also the renowned wrecking Of the East Indiaman, Earl of Abergavenny, which sank 2 miles off Weymouth beach. 300 people died, and 200 of them were buried in Wyke Regis Church yard.

In 1809 'the grateful inhabitants' of Weymouth subscribed to have erected the King's Statue at the north end of St. Thomas and St. Mary Street, in recognition of His Majesty's contribution to the wealth and standing of the town. It was not at that time painted, but was built in artificial stone. It was not until 1949 that it was painted, a most unusual and curiously pleasing step. Another and more curious commemoration in 1808 of George III was the cutting out in chalk of the king on horseback, riding forever on a hill in Osmington overlooking the bay. The king lived on, sick and sequestered, until 1820.

In 1824 the Esplanade was destroyed by a tempest, as a commemorative table on the Esplanade records. 1824 also saw the building of a stone Town Bridge, with a swinging section, on the present day site.

It will be seen from what has gone before that attention had been drawn away from the commercial port of Weymouth, but in 1794 a Packet Service was undertaken between Weymouth and Channel Islands.

The fishing fleet also flourished thanks to better road links with the outside world, all this being accompanied by a substantial increase in population, Unfortunately there was no way in which the port could continue to grow; in an age of larger ships it was a case of larger ports.

The mid-1800s witnessed another substantial growth in new building. The Portwey Hospital started life as a workhouse in 1836, and although now converted to flats, is a handsome stone building; Holy Trinity Church, facing the Town Bridge was opened in the same year, and 1838 the Guildhall was opened. 1854 was the year which St. John's Church was built at Greenhill.

The reclamation of land from the Backwater and Radipole Lake was by now being taken very seriously; the present day railway station, for example, and Commercial Road along which the line to the ferries run, bowling green and the very large car park (present day Thursday Market) are all built on land that was once the Backwater.

1770-1824 Wooden Town Bridge which crossed Weymouth Harbour

"THE OSMINGTON HORSE"

The Osmington White Horse which overlooks Weymouth Bay, in Dorset, is another comparatively recent example of confusion. There are three suggestions put forward for the carving of this horse.

The first view is that it was carved by a soldier to commemorate the visits made to Weymouth by George fit and his brother, the Duke of Gloucester.

Another explanation is that it was created by engineers expecting a Napoleonic invasion. Though precisely what good they thought the carving would do is doubtful.

The final conjecture is that it was excavated by enthusiastic navvies celebrating the British victory at Trafalgar. This last idea was put forward by Thomas Hardy in 'The Trumpet Major'.

This is now generally accepted to be the figure of George III and to have been carved around 1815. The story is that he was extremely annoyed by this portrayal as it's pointing away from Weymouth. The King took this to mean that he was no longer welcome there, and so never returned again.

TRAINS AND TRIPPERS

The railway was late in coming to Weymouth, 1857 in fact, and it was in two gauges in order to accommodate the two railway companies, the GWR and the LSWR. The line to Portland was opened in 1865, with the first train arriving half an hour late!

There were mixed feelings about the railway's arrival. Previously Weymouth appealed to the more genteel market, and it was felt that the humbler sort of people, provided with easy rail access, would lower the tone. Whatever the case the new rail link, ending in huge gaunt sheds, provided not only a lot of direct employment but gave rise to a massive increase in building. A great many houses along the Esplanade, hitherto private homes, now provided accommodation. The age of the tripper was coming.

The Sands, Jubilee Clock Tower and Esplanade

The sandy beach, substantial as it was, was further extended by the continued growth of the pier on the Melcombe Regis side, thus making the sandy beach into an elegant curve.

Trips along the coast to Lulworth were very popular, but this popularity was overtaken in 1849 to see the Portland Breakwater being built. It had long been suggested that such a breakwater would provide Portland Harbour with a sound defence behind which warships could anchor and be serviced and supplied in comparative safety. In 1849 work was begun on the two breakwaters, while those from the Weymouth side were not begun until 1890. The success of the breakwaters exceeded expectations and many warships could take refuge for refits and rests within its confines. The material used was inferior capstone from Portland quarries, trundled out to its destination by long trains staging, with gaps between sleepers through which material could be tipped.

In spite of the continuing growth of the town and its appeal to holiday makers, sanitation was appalling, little changed from medieval times. Muck was collected and tipped into the sea and open gutters and sewers ran down the streets. Typhoid was a continual hazard. The dam built across Radipole Lake was intended to periodically wash away accumulated rubbish, but the inevitable result was a worsening of the situation. Fresh water was not available until 1855, from large springs at Sutton Poyntz; previously water had been obtainable only from a limited number of pumps, taps and wells and even these supplies were rationed.

The 1850s and 60s were marked by more building schemes. The Park area, north of the railway station ·filled in the large triangle of land formed by the Esplanade on one side, the railway terminus on another and the Dorchester

Road on the third. The buildings behind the King's Statue were also erected at this time, thus forming the entrance to the two main streets as we see today. The districts of Westham, Chickerell and Pye Hill were connected to Weymouth by the first Westham Bridge, a toll road built on piers. It was not until 1921 that this was replaced and Radipole Lake formed by the provision of sluices in the bridge, rendering the lake no longer tidal.

Harbour dredging was carried out substantially and the pier was yet further extended. Paddle steamers and sailing boats used the pier for the handling of both cargoes and passengers using the rather spasmodic French ferries, and by 1889 the Weymouth Harbour Tramway, horse drawn and later steam powered, had reached the landing stage for the ferries.

By now, the mid 1800s, Portland was established as a major naval port. Breakwaters were being built to protect Portland Roads and part of these defences was the building of the Nothe Fort. There had been fortifications on this headland for several hundred years, including the small fort from which the cannon ball mentioned at the beginning derived, but this was a massive affair, completed in 1872, and is a place well worth visiting today. It was originally armed with 10 large guns and two lighter ones, but the only time the Fort saw action was during the Second World War, when its armament was anti-aircraft guns.

By 1880 several of the gardens which contribute so much to Weymouth's charms were established, even the Nothe being laid out with walls, flower beds and shrubs, a tradition which persists today. The Alexandra Gardens followed, and later still, in recent years, gardens were set out along the steep embankment behind the Municipal Offices. One can walk among flower colour all the way from Greenhill to Alexandra Gardens, and hanging bowls of flowers are

The Nothe Hill and Fort from the Quay

13

set on lamp standards along the main road. Few seaside towns are as pretty or as well maintained, and the recently pedestrianised St Mary Street is a real delight.

By Alexandra Gardens is a statue to the long serving MP Sir Henry Edwards, and it was he who paid for the Jubilee Clock on the Esplanade, erected 1887 for the Golden Jubilee of Queen Victoria.

The early years of the 20th century saw more changes. Land reclamation was still being practised using waste Portland stone, but some local industries were ceasing. Templeman's Crown Flour Mills burnt down in 1917, coal handling in the harbour ended as did the handling of cement and timber, the latter meaning that the tall ships of the Baltic became figures of the past. King George VI, as Duke of York in 1930, opened the present Town Bridge.

Besides its popularity as a resort Weymouth had a lot to offer yachtsmen of the day. G. A. Henty died on board his yacht in 1903, while Sir Thomas Lipton used Weymouth Bay as training waters for his America's Cup contenders Shamrock I and III.

THE WAR

During the First World War Weymouth hosted many Commonwealth and American troops, and became a centre for medical and rehabilitation work, but in other ways was not so closely affected by the first war as by the second.

World War II saw evacuees arriving from Dunkirk, and very shortly afterwards the first of many bombs fell. In August 1940 came the first heavy bombing raid which caused considerable damage and loss of life.

Many buildings along the Esplanade had deep cellars, and although little damage occurred in this particular area much use was made of these cellars as shelters.

In 1944 much of the South coast and Weymouth in particular, was occupied by Allied forces preparing for the Normandy Landings, with over half a million troops being embarked, along with transport and tanks. This is remembered by a memorial opposite the Royal Hotel. At the end of the war German U Boat U249 was brought into Weymouth Bay, the first of the German submarines to do so.

Now, in the years of peace, the Pier Bandstand which had been opened just before World War II could come into use. It lasted until 1986 when the structure over the sea was demolished, having become unsafe. A local major business which had been badly damaged during the war was the Devenish Brewery, but its Hope Square business came back into production. In 1954 the old and ornate Pavilion Theatre was destroyed by fire, but was later re-opened in 1960.

Weymouth today is caught between two choices, whether to expand and industrialise, which will involve building on the surrounding farmlands, or remain a tourist town with a declining role.

PART II

PORTLAND

The Isle of Portland extends dramatically into the Channel, forming the most southerly protrusion of the West Dorset coast. It is a solid block of limestone, one immense quarry, measuring 4 1/2 miles long and 1 '/2 miles wide, with a circumference of 9 miles.

Prior to the construction of The Ferry Bridge in 1839, Portland was connected to the mainland only by the great arm of the Chesil Bank, stretching parallel to the Dorset coastline for 16 miles, before meeting the main beach at Abbotsbury. Between the Bank and the main coast lies the Fleet.

The origin of this unique beach is unknown, although many theories have been speculated upon. The long smooth ridge of pebbles presents a marked contrast to the rocky and charming coves to be discovered on the Isle, many of which resemble the smaller beaches of the Cornish coast. South westerly gales are held responsible for the increasing size of pebbles moving to the east, resulting in the shingle at Portland being large, whilst the stones towards the Bridport direction become gradually smaller. The sea rarely crosses over the ridge of shingle, but the occasion of a storm is a most dramatic and thrilling sight. The notorious storm of 1824 destroyed much of the small village of Fleet (a couple of miles west of Weymouth), plus houses on the west coast of Portland, and some of Weymouth. A 'tidal' wave in 1924 also swept away part of, and severely flooded, Chiswell on Portland.

Despite its link with the mainland however, Portland remained very much an island, protecting its unique community and existence fiercely throughout the ages, the invasions and inevitable outside attempts to revolutionise or

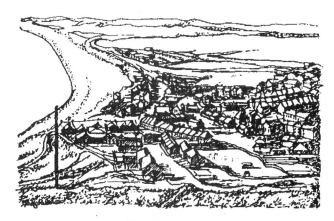

The Chesil Bank

reform life there. As early as the 1530's, John Leland, visiting the Isle of Portland, .remarked upon the strong, wilful, "somewhat avaricious" inhabitants there, mentioning also their skill in slinging stones, a practice to which they resorted fairly frequently. The isle was, and in many ways remains, self sufficient, with a government, resources and economy secure enough to allow it to be independent. Strangers seldom went there and even more rarely settled there, hence it was populated by a few families whose members frequently intermarried; names such as Stone, Pearce, Comben and White were most common. Understandably, with only a handful of surnames scattered around the Isle, matters became confused, as many also had the same Christian names! Hence most inhabitants of Portland had a nickname to distinguish them from their brethren. Even until fairly recent times, neighbours were always known as 'Aunt and Uncle'. Hence visits from strangers "kimberluns" · were regarded with suspicion and hostility, stemming perhaps from the Portlander's reluctance to accept interference and change when the Isle offered all he could need.

Quarrying of the stone of which Portland is made had been carried out for centuries, becoming a marketable enterprise in the 17th century, and most people were employed in some way in the industry. If work was slack however, there was no problem about resorting to fishing or farming, which until the mid 19th century had provided the main source of employment. The Portlanders were united by strange, durable ties created by their shared myths, beliefs and customs. Their faith in the supernatural was as strong as their religious beliefs; when Methodism became popular on Portland, they were told they could not worship at the Church and believe in witchcraft too. The sensible Portlanders, not wishing to sacrifice one belief for another, built themselves another Chapel which allowed them worship both God and retain the faith that formed the integral part of the structure of life on the "island".

Any stranger disrespectful of the customs and rights of the Portlanders very quickly found himself pelted with hard clods of earth, or pieces of stone which lay liberally around the Island. The Portlanders were no gentle race either, described by Hutchins as: "a stout, hardy, industrious race... very healthy but not long lived, for though at 60 many of the men appear strong and robust, they soon drop off, and there are no instances of longevity, which may be accounted for from too great a use of spirits".

Thomas Hardy used Portland as the location for his novel "The Well Beloved", calling it "The Isle of the slingers". He described it as, "carved by time out of a single stone", and the home of; "a curious and almost distinctive people, cherishing strange beliefs and irregular customs".

THE CHARACTER OF PORTLAND

Portland's landscape is completely unique. It is an island of contrasts. At the northern end it rises to a steep 496 feet, forming the areas known as Underhill and Tophill, whilst at the southerly end, Portland Bill (or Beale as it was known) is only 20 feet above the water.

The quarrying of the past centuries have destroyed evidence of the farming system used, but the medieval methods survived throughout agricultural practice, when places on the mainland had long since abandoned them.

Almost devoid of trees and bearing the scars of constant quarrying everywhere, Portland can appear a bleak and grim place, but paradoxically, it's beauty and strength lies in that starkness, caves still bear great boulders of white stone that appear to have been tossed down, unused from the quarries above, whilst old cottages, built by individuals from stone left lying around, are unique and exquisite in character, with low roofs and great slabs for porches. In contrast are the great timeless rows of Victorian terraces, imposing and cold in their white stone, reminding us of the great buildings of London that Portland stone created. The Island appears both threatening and reassuring in its abandonment and beauty. One can easily understand the reluctance to admit "progression" into this place of energy and tradition.

Inevitably change had to occur. The building of the Ferry Bridge in 1839, allowed easier access to and from Portland, and its resources were quickly recognised. In 1851, the population of the Island was 5,195 · by 1901 it had risen by 10,000. Rail in the 19th century revolutionised life on the Island and enabled the quarrying business to extend nationally. Gradually the Island looked on the mainland for services such as water, gas, electricity, and eventually these became centralised.

The real changes occurred during the past century, with advanced technology recognising Portland's ideal position of defence, and the locating on the Island of naval institutions, bringing many newcomers. Ironically, the Island's position of isolation made her an ideal place to locate a fortress and a prison. A further irony lies in the fact that the convicts built the Verne Fortress which later became the present day prison, the site of the old one now used as a Reform School.

The fierce opposition on Portland since prehistoric times however, was not to succumb easily to forces of more recent times. The Romans had invaded the isle, but failed to monopolise the spirit of its inhabitants; the Danes, Saxons and Normans all appear to have made little impact upon the great slab of limestone at the end of the mainland · or perhaps they saw little scope there.

The Upper Lighthouse and Cliffs near Portland Bill

The democratic souls of Portland were quick to react to any threat, calling a public meeting instantly. At one such meeting in January 1866, the Local Government Act of 1858 was accepted, only to be violently opposed by petition the following year. Much stormy debating followed, and the Portlanders finally saw the sense in the change. In more recent times, the suggestion of a Union between Portland and Weymouth brought an extreme response, and in 1971, Portland proposed a Unilateral Declaration of Independence, which would have made it similar to Gibraltar, having it's own passports, tax laws, etc. Unfortunately the battle was lost, and Portland became united with Weymouth on April 1st, 1974. Being united administratively with the mainland however, did not mean Portland had to change its inherently insular way of life, nor did it relinquish its manorial system of government, which had survived since the Saxon Ages.

LIFE ON PORTLAND

Access from the mainland to Portland is by way of The Ferry Bridge, which extends at Smallmouth from the main A354. From this point, the great Chesil Bank stretches to the west, Weymouth lies to the east, whilst the great hunk of oolitic limestone, Portland, looms ahead.

The first Ferry Bridge was constructed in 1839, although petitioning and pleading was happening at the turn of the century, requesting the King's permission for a safe bridge to replace the precarious crossing made by ferry. The museum on Portland had a replica of the prices charged by the ferry, ranging from 1d for a foot passenger, to 3s and 6d for a coach. The great storm of 1824, which claimed many things, including the ferryman's life, urged an act to be passed in July 1835 for the bridge to be built. Tolls were to be paid by all users, excepting the Royal Family, Armed forces and Royal Mail.

Use of the road today is free, and leads across the high stretch of Chesil shingle, past former naval establishments and the massive helicopter base, once the tidal mere wherein the sheep of the island were washed. The road meets Portland at the Northern end, steering around to Castletown on the left and rising steeply through Chiswell and Fortuneswell ahead. At one time, the island consisted of small, separate villages and hamlets, each separated by a 'greenbelt'. The lower, northern part of the Isle is the more 'cosmopolitan' and known as underhill. Its status probably arose from its nearness to the mainland · visitors would often assume that nothing lay on tophill except a few shepherds' cottages. A few mysterious myths grew around the unseen higher land. Some folks from underhill claimed that those from tophill had tails, whilst the people from tophill didn't consider those below to be 'true' Portlanders!

Despite their indifference to newcomers and antagonism towards authority, Portland was one of the few places that remained loyal to the crown. The Island belongs to the crown, who as absent lord of the Manor, continues to appoint officers of the Manor that has existed since Saxon times. The absenteeism of a lord of the Manor resulted in a self government and democracy still prevalent to-day, and islanders retained rights over their houses and land and the stone quarried from the island. They were on amicable terms with Royalty, accepting the due privileges bestowed upon them in return for their loyalty, and welcoming the regular visits from George III at the end of the 8th century.

The manorial system has inevitably lost some of its powers, but remains an active institution, covering all aspects of life on the island, meeting twice a year, still having a jury of 24 tenants of the Isle. On Ascension Day, every seven years the Bounds are beaten on the Boundary stone, which can be seen on a clear day from Ferry Bridge, along the Chesil Beach near Abbotsbury.

At Michaelmas Court, a Reeve was chosen, whose job it was to collect the rents. The job only ever lasted one year. Rents were incredibly low, the Portlanders having retained ancient rights concerning property. Firstly, there was common land, on which anyone could raise livestock, and the threat of enclosure was never accepted on Portland. Secondly, land could be transferred by one of three means · it could be given from one party to another as a church gift; it could be surrendered at court; it could be left in a will · if there was no will, the land was divided equally between a man's wife and sons. Inevitably this led to many people owning lots of small bits of land. Enclosure would have destroyed the livelihood of the smaller concerns, and besides, was finally decided to be much too expensive, as there were so many pieces of land to enclose! A simple answer to any attempt at enclosure would have been to tear the boundaries down !

Many people on the Isle built their own houses on their land, from redundant stone left around. The Reeve recorded his rents collected on a staff, made usually from mahogany or pine coneuras reputedly made from silver, salvaged from a Spanish Armada). They were between 7 and 12 feet in length, and a series of notches and symbols indicated what had been collected · a whole notch represented a shilling, whereas a 1/4 Of a scratch stood for a farthing! The five areas of Portland · Wakeham, Southwell, Easton, Weston and Chiswell each had their own mark. The rents were duly presented at the court leet and dinner followed at The Lugger Inn, renowned both for being a smugglers haunt, and the first house on Portland to have real glass windows! The Reeve earned £1.00 a year for his troubles. The Court met at The George Inn, the old clerks house, which has a Reeve's Staff on show and is well worth a visit. A Staff is also present in The Museum.

The names of the villages in Portland indicate that wells provided the source of water on the Island. The pond became the central aspect of each area. In Easton Square, where there are now gardens laid out, was once the parish pump, and previous to this, the village pond, filled in 1873 Weston pond was also filled in the early 20th century, due to its smelly and dangerous state. Easton was in previous times, the hub of life on Tophill, and people rarely ventured down the steep path to the lower villages, except for the annual fair held during a few days around November 6th, which acted as a social pulley, winding all the inhabitants of the isle together. It was held originally in Fortuneswell, moving to Chiswell; in 1860, the cattle market and amusements were separated, and in the present day, the annual fun fair is a major event on Portland.

Lives revolved around the work contained in the small surrounding area, resources were shared. People lived in close reverence of forces greater

19

than themselves, and most had a Bay Tree in the garden to guard against witches. A peculiar custom some years ago was the acceptance that a man and woman married only when the woman was already with child. She informed her mother, who informed her father, who informed the boy's father, who informed his son that it was time to get married! As this custom was always respected, there were virtually no cases of illegitimacy on the Island. Visitors who got themselves into a sticky situation without realising it's effect were stoned violently from the island.

Until the 19th century, most schooling probably took place in local houses, and the census returns of 1851 reveal that there was only one Governess on the island The earliest recorded school was situated where Tophill library, Easton, is now, and was known as The Straits, or The Masters Rooms, after a popular schoolmaster, Master Harry. Even after the school rooms became a social room, the Portlanders, impermeable to change, continued to refer to it as "The Masters Room". In the early 19th century, schools began to emerge around the island, often having more male than female attendants.

INDUSTRY: AGRICULTURE AND QUARRYING

A trip around the Isle of Portland reveals many disused quarry sites and dumping grounds. At one time there were over a hundred quarries operating people had every right to simply begin their own business on private land;

Portland 'Lerret' a local sea boat ideal for the rough conditions off Portland

now the business has become more centralised. At one point recently, a suggestion was made that the disused quarry sites be used as a dumping ground for old cars of Dorset - it was understandably given a violent elbow by the people of Portland. To appreciate the way of working on the Island, one must be aware that its economy was illegitimacy on the Island. Visitors who got themselves sufficient meant that a peasant in mainland terms was somebody with possession in Portland terms. People could return to fishing or farming if times were hard, and live off fish if food was short, and ship share timber (from wrecks) was constantly available for fuel.

Agriculture remained a predominant occupation until the quarrying war encroached upon it both economically and physically. Areas on the Island were divided into fields, North, South, East and West, and one was always left fallow for a year. This rather uneconomical system was related to a shortage of manure; dung from cattle was often used as fuel - there was a shortage of trees on the island - thus another strange practice evolved. Urine was collected during the summer months, and put on the crops during the winter. (The crop would be destroyed if it was distributed in hot weather) The land however was

20

fertile, producing wheat, barley and corn. Two windmill stumps can still be seen south west of Easton Square. They were called cotton fields and Top Growlands, and were probably used from the 17th century until the end of the 19th century.

John Leland, visiting Portland in the 16th century, remarked upon the great quantity of sheep present. The Portland sheep were a rare, small horned breed which unfortunately disappeared during this century. However, the Rare Breeds Trust helped its survival by reintroducing the breed back to the island in 1977.

Stone quarrying had probably existed on Portland since the 14th century, but gained fame during the 17th century. It was used by Inigo Jones, the Architect of James I, for the Banqueting Hall at Whitehall, and the exportation of Portland stone began.

A pier was constructed at the beginning of the 17th century, and stone was used for repairing many buildings in London following the Great Fire of 1666. The tenants of Portland were entitled to a percentage of the 1 shilling levy paid on every ton of stone exported, and the proceeds were divided equally between the crown and Portlanders. (Stone for the crown's sole use however, did not pay any duty). In 1675, a dispute arose, Charles II had allowed Christopher Wren to export stone for the building of St. Paul's Cathedral, and queries arose as to whether this stone was for the crown's use or not. In return for their loyalty to the Crown, Charles granted an extra 3d on each ton of stone hewed from the island, so the tenants received 9d, the Crown 3d.

The new industry inevitably brought migrants to the Isle, but the Portland workers did not concern themselves with the risks taken by the large merchants (many goods were lost at sea and bad debts incurred); they simply got on with their jobs. One islander remembers the quarrymen going to work with their flasks of cold tea, describing them: "As durable as Portland Stone". These hard working folk were often drinking men, stopping for a pint or so on route to work (pubs opened at 6.00 a.m.), and sending a boy back for another gallon during the day.

A hazardous two-horse braking system was used to transfer the stone to the harbours, until in 1826, the merchants' railway, running from Priory Corner down to Castletown, was constructed, designed by James Brown. It was just over 2 miles long, and operated on a system of the full carts going down pulling the empty ones up.

A great superstition revolved around the rabbits, which quarrymen held responsible for burrowing through the Island, thus making the quarries unsafe. It reached the extreme at one point of forcing a quarryman to return home if one was in his path, and is still a joke on the island.

From 1865 until 1965, the main railway extended to Portland. The first station was in Victoria Square, whilst Easton Station opened in 1902. This scenic route from Chiswell had taken 14 years to complete and is remembered as a splendidly dramatic journey along the steep inclines of the coast. Portland gradually saw the outside world transgressing its boundaries.

The merchants' railway was discontinued in 1939.

21

PORTLAND ROLE OF DEFENCE

In the 1500's, Henry VIII commissioned a line of defence to be constructed along the South West Coast of England, fearing retaliation from the Pope's armies following his dissolution of the monasteries. Portland Castle stood in relation to Sandsfoot Castle, across the water at Wyke Regis and was completed in the 1530's. Sandsfoot castle has long since fallen into decay, but Portland remains well preserved, and is open to the public throughout the summer. It is worth a visit, as access to the harbour, now used by naval and military organisations, is denied, and one has to go to the higher part of the island to gain a bird's eye view. A meticulous account of expenditure was kept, the consequent cost of building amounting to £4964.19s.10 3/4d. The walls are over a foot thick in places. Henry VIII bestowed the castle at different times to three of his wives.

During the Civil War (1642 1646), the castle was garrisoned by the Parliamentarians in the outset, retaken by the Royalist forces in 1643. By 1645, the Parliamentarians were victorious in the towns of Melcombe Regis and Weymouth, and regained possession of Portland, although the Castle refused to surrender to the forces until the following year. Portland has remained fiercely Royalist - perhaps relating to its reluctance to admit change. Portland had witnessed a fierce sea battle in the year of 1588, when on May 23rd, English ships clashed with the galleons of the Spanish Armada. By the mid C 19th, the decision was made to credit a deep anchorage harbour at Portland for the navy's massive ships, and in 1849, the first stone of the Portland Breakwater was laid by Prince Albert, the patron of the Island. 23 years later, the completing stone was placed by his son, the Prince of Wales, later King Edward VII. The massive Verne fortress, carved partly out of the Island itself, was also constructed.

Convict labour was used to do the hard, back breaking work. On 21st November, 1848, the first group of convicts arrived, and soon, over 500 a day were working in the quarries. Speaking was not permitted, and separate quarries and rail were used than those of the merchants. The prisoners wore arrowed suits, and few escaped, although local legend recalls one who hid in the crypt of a Roman Chapel, happily drinking brandy and smoking cigars. Unfortunately he overslept on the day of the planned escape, and was traced by the pungent odours he had created!

The prison was developed not solely for the use of convict labour, but also as part of a scheme which allowed people sentenced to transportation to do one year in a closed prison, learning a skill, which would enable them to lead a better life when their sentence had been served. William Forsyth, visiting the prison in 1873, was impressed by the healthy lifestyle, the "exquisitely clean". rooms and "beautifully kept harness room". He neglects to mention the many instruments of torture, and the 20 attempted suicides in the year of 1883.

St. Peter's Church in The Grove, near the former prison, was also built by convicts, and contains exhibits of Mosaic work by Constance Kent, a descendent of the Duke of Kent, imprisoned for murdering her brother. The museum contains an excellent engraving on slate, done by a convict who was a bank note forger!

The former prison is now a reform school, an imposing white stone building on the eastern side of the Island, offering magnificent views of Purbeck Cliffs. There are footpaths from here too, but don't wait when the red flag is flying!

The Verne, built by former convicts, is the prison today. With the completion of the Breakwater enclosing the Naval harbour, Portland became a base for many naval and military forces, creating a mass influx bringing with it mass culture. Underhill grew rapidly and the Victorian era saw the creation of many gun batteries still in existence today.

Standing above Fortuneswell Iust below the Portland Heights Hotel (follow New Road out of Fortuneswell), offers the most magnificent view of the Harbour, Weymouth, and across the Chesil Beach, reaching out in the distance like a great golden snake in the sea. Immediately below, the cottages of underhill descend steeply into the area of Chiswell and Fortuneswell.

TOPHILL, WAKEHAM, SOUTHWELL AND PORTLAND BILL

Wakeham was the most populated part of the Island during the 18th century. John Penn, Governor of the Island and descendant of William Penn, founder of Pennsylvania, owned some property there. Some 200 years before, a beautiful building, perhaps a chapel or vicar's house, is believed to have existed, long since destroyed, probably in the Civil War.

At the end of the row of stone slab porched cottages in Wakeham is the museum, established in 1929, founded by Marie Stopes, who lived in the upper lighthouse on The Bill. The museum was the cottage named by Thomas Hardy in his novel "The Well Beloved" as "Avices Cottage"

The footpath running beside the museum winds past cafes, beneath the Georgian bridge that leads to the remains of Rufus Castle, or Bow and Arrow Castle. The ledge here overlooks Church Ope Cave, and is one of the most beautiful places on the Island.

Beyond, the blue of the sea contrasts against the white of the stones. Steps lead down to the tiny cove flanked by beach huts, whilst paths venture across the rough and rocky land to the edge of the cliffs. The chalky white cliffs of the Purbeck Hills can be seen on the left, whilst behind, the sheer edge of the Cliff face rises sharply to support the ruins of Rufus Castle.

Although the Castle was probably built initially during the reign of William Rufus, it is more likely to have acquired its name from The Red Earl, Robert of Gloucester, who took the Castle in 1142, during the Civil War between Stephen and Matilda, who reputedly escaped during the winter-time, camouflaged by a white night-gown!

The castle was rebuilt in the mid 15th century by Richard, Duke of York, although little remains of it today.

To the left of the Castle, lie the ruins of St. Andrew's Church, carefully reconstructed (many original stones and headstones are in the garden of the museum). The Church probably stood on the site of a former Saxon Church, and was in a decayed state by 1745. In 1573, the decision was made to build a new place of worship for the Island, and a temporary tabernacle was erected in

Wakeham whilst St. George's (Weston Road) was erected. St. George's suffered a boggy graveyard and damage from storms in 1795, but was restored in recent years, and now forms an impressive sight in its solitary position, looking out to sea.

Churches were growing throughout the 19th century, as Methodism became popular, but the non-conformity characteristic of Portland remains evident in both architecture and their refusal to give up the 'pagan' beliefs which had existed for centuries past. (The Grave was believed to be the site of pagan, pre-Christian ceremonies).

From St. Andrews, a small path leads into the ruins, to the right from the steps to Church Ope Cave. The Portland Stone graves bear dates of 1700's - it is a thrilling feeling to stand above the cove once frequented by smugglers, amidst a desolate and ruined Church.

Behind St. Andrews looms Pennsylvania Hotel, built by John Penn in 1800 at a cost of £2,000, as a private residence. The Portlanders were not happy at being rearranged to make way for his whims, and demonstrated their opposition by tearing down the walls! The Quarry Stone Grant footed the bill for expenses incurred in the dispute between the Court leet and Mr. Penn, who later took an active interest in the affairs of the Island.

Portland Bill is the most southerly point of the Island, an open, blustery fresh, expanse of land looking out to sea. Here there is a lighthouse, open to the public, and a variety of cafes and stalls.

There were originally 2 lighthouses situated on the Bill, lit at first by coal, and later by rows of oil lamps. In 1789, one was rebuilt in a different position, and in 1869, both were rebuilt.

The lower one is now the Bird Observatory and Field Centre. The present lighthouse was erected in 1908. Portland is surrounded by danger zones - The Shambles, a 4 mile long band of sand lies south-east of the Bill, whilst south-east of St. Andrews, two tides meet and form a whirlpool of uneven depths at a place called The Race. Not surprisingly, wrecks were an almost weekly occurrence.

As all seamen, Portlanders were eager to rescue their fellow men, and subsequently keen to plunder their vessels! Smuggling was rife - one contraband turned guardsman admitted that whilst sending smugglers off to Dorchester Courts, they themselves indulged in smuggled goods!

Pulpit Rock, a strange geological formation, has always been associated with smuggling exploits, marking the entrance to numerous small caves, 'Cave Hole' being the largest at 50ft by 20ft. "Brandy Row" leading down to Chiswell Cove has long since been demolished, but its name needs no explanation!

The 19th and 20th centuries have taken their toll on the Isle of Portland, and it bears little resemblance today to the landscape drawings and paintings of Samuel Grimm and John Upham, exhibited in the Museum. Speaking to local people, it is easier to understand their wish to protect the freedom of their home and lives.